D0542667

An introduction to British trees: a photographic gu

WITHDRAWN

111882

Non-Fiction 582.16 GOG

Wycliffe College

THE LIBRARY
Wycliffe College Stonehouse
Gloucestershire, GL10 2JQ
Tel: 01453-820438

An Introduction to British Trees

A Photographic Guide

Liz Gogerly
Photographs by Archie Miles

WAYLAND

This book is a differentiated text version of *The Wayland Book of Common British Trees* by Theresa Greenaway

First published in Great Britain in 2006 by Wayland,
an imprint of Hachette Children's Books

Hachette Children's Books
338 Euston Road, London NW1 3BH

© Copyright 2006 Wayland

All rights reserved. Apart from any use permitted under UK copyright law, this publication may only be reproduced, stored or transmitted, in any form, or by any means with prior permission in writing of the publishers or in the case of reprographic production in accordance with the terms of licences issued by the Copyright Licensing Agency.

Editor: Camilla Lloyd
Senior Design Manager: Rosamund Saunders
Designer: Jane Hawkins
Photographer: Archie Miles

Archie Miles gratefully acknowledges the assistance of Westonbirt Arboretum, Gloucestershire; Queenswood Arboretum, Herefordshire; The Foley Estate; Hergest Croft Gardens; Emmy Johnson (planting seedling); Trees for London (urban tree planting).

Cover photograph: Ancient holly tree on the Stiperstones in Shropshire (Castanea sativa).
Title page: A common oak (Quercus robur).
This page (from top): Winter buds of a horse chestnut twig; spindle in fruit; crab apple blossom; hawthorn berries.
Contents page (from top): A crack willow; an old pollard hornbeam; an ancient holly tree with berries; a sweet chestnut.

Gogerly, Liz
An introduction to British trees
1.Trees - Great Britain - Identification - Juvenile literature
I.Title
582.1'6'0941

ISBN-10: 0-7502-4991-9
ISBN-13: 978-0-7502-4991-1

Printed and bound in China

The website addresses (URLs) included in this book were valid at the time of going to press. However, because of the nature of the Internet, it is possible that some addresses may have changed, or sites may have changed or closed down since publication. While the author and publisher regret any inconvenience this may cause the readers, no responsibility for any such changes can be accepted by either the author or the publisher.

Contents

What are Trees?

There are hundreds of different kinds of trees growing in Britain. They are very important to people, animals and the environment. Trees provide us with wood and food like fruits and nuts. They give animals food too and a place to nest.

PARTS OF TREES

Trees have a woody stem called a trunk. The trunk has many leafy branches. Fruits can grow on the branches. Seeds are made inside the fruit. Trees also have roots that grow deep into the soil. These are important because they provide water and food. Trees must have food and water to grow.

WHAT ARE SHRUBS?

Shrubs are mostly smaller than trees. They do not have a single trunk. They have lots of woody branches that grow near the ground.

GROUPS OF TREES

Trees are divided into three groups. There are broadleaved trees, conifer trees and palm trees. In Britain we have mainly broadleaved and conifer trees. Palm trees usually grow in warmer regions of the world.

▶ *The hazel is a shrub. Can you see the branches near the ground?*

◀ *The field oak is a tree. It has a large trunk.*

Broadleaved trees have broad, flat leaves. They also have flowers that become fruits.

Conifers mostly have hard, narrow leaves called needles. Conifers do not have flowers. The seeds for these trees are found in cones or cups.

Palm trees have one woody trunk. Their leaves are very large. These are found in a cluster at the top of the tree. Palm trees also have flowers.

▼ *The ash is a broadleaved tree.*

▼ *The Scots pine is a conifer.*

▼ *This palm tree is growing on an island in the Caribbean.*

DECIDUOUS TREES

Some trees drop all their leaves in the autumn. These are called deciduous trees. They shed their leaves to protect them from the harsh winter weather. Frost and snow would damage leaves. Branches with leaves can be blown down easily too. Before the tree sheds its leaves, the leaves pass their nutrients back to the branches. This is why leaves change colour in the autumn.

EVERGREEN TREES

Trees that keep their leaves all through the winter are called evergreen. The leaves of the evergreen are tough and will not blow down easily.

▲ *The red oak has bright red and orange leaves in autumn.*

▶ *Insects like butterflies and bees carry pollen from one flower to another.*

FROM SEED TO TREE

Trees start their life as seeds. The seeds grow into saplings before becoming adult trees. The seeds of a tree grow in the female part of the plant. This might be a flower or a female cone. Seeds need pollen to grow. Pollen comes from the male part of a plant called the male cone. Pollen is carried to the seed by wind or insects. This process is called pollination.

SPREADING THE SEED

Trees spread their seeds in different ways. Some trees have winged fruits or seeds covered in fine cotton hairs. These seeds can be caught by the wind and spread over a wide area. Birds can also spread seeds. They eat the berries or fruits on trees. The seeds inside the fruit are spread in the birds' droppings.

▲ *The field maple has winged fruit. The wind can carry the fruit a long way.*

▶ *Birds like to eat these tasty red hawthorn berries. The seeds of the hawthorn are carried in the berries.*

White willow

Scientific name: *Salix alba*	Native
Height: up to 25 metres	
Bark: dark grey, diamond-shaped ridges	

The white willow looks pale when you look at it from a distance. This is because its leaves have white hairs on both sides. Its leaves are long and narrow. The white willow's tiny flowers are bunched together in catkins. The white willow likes damp soil and is often found beside rivers, streams and ponds.

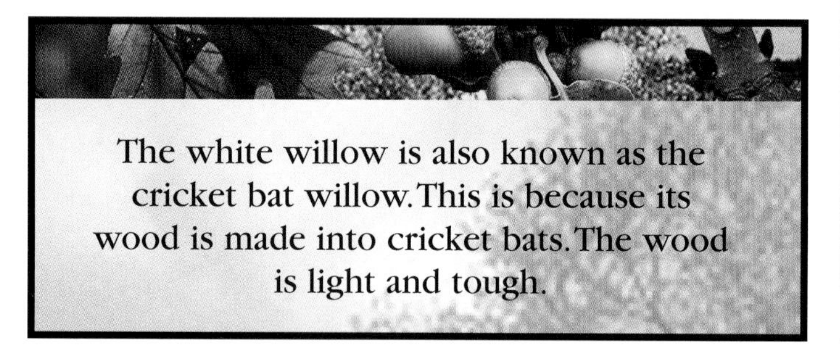

The white willow is also known as the cricket bat willow. This is because its wood is made into cricket bats. The wood is light and tough.

▲ *White willows have tall crowns and pale leaves.*

Weeping willow

Scientific name: *Salix x sepulcralis*	Hybrid
Height: up to 10 metres	
Bark: pale greyish-brown, ridged	

The weeping willow has long slender leaves and long shoots which hang straight down. These shoots nearly touch the ground and sway in the wind.

The weeping willow is a hybrid. This means that it is a cross between two different kinds of willow tree. The weeping willow is a cross between the white willow and the Chinese weeping willow.

◀ *The weeping willow is often planted near ponds and rivers. Its leaves nearly touch the water.*

Pussy willow or sallow

Scientific name: *Salix caprea*	**Native**
Height: up to 10 metres	
Bark: smooth, pale grey with small diamond-shaped cracks	

The pussy willow has catkins that are covered in soft whitish fur. This fur feels like cat's fur, which is how the tree got its name.

This small tree has oval, pointed leaves. It flowers in spring.

▶ *Pussy willow catkins are one of the first signs of spring.*

Osier

Scientific name: *Salix viminalis*	**Native**
Height: up to 6 metres	
Bark: greyish-brown, becoming cracked with age	

The osier is a willow tree. It mostly grows in waterlogged ground as a thicket. The osier has thin leaves with edges that are rolled under.

◀ *The shoots of the osier are long and straight. They can grow as much as 2.5 metres in a year.*

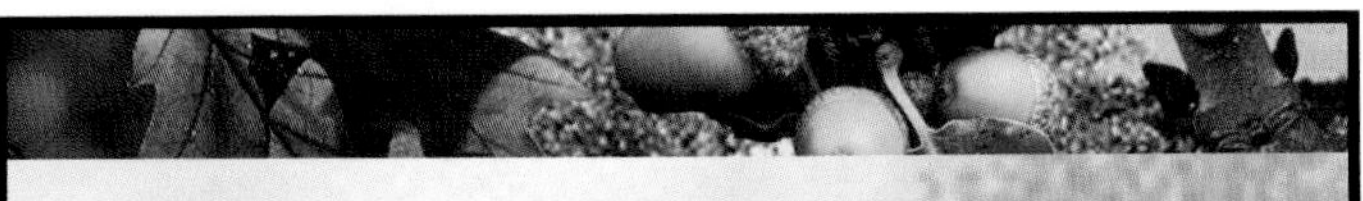

The long straight shoots of the osier are perfect for weaving into baskets. They are grown in osier beds. Each year the shoots are cut back to ground level. Many new shoots grow the next year.

Crack willow

Scientific name: *Salix fragilis*	**Native**
Height: up to 15 metres	
Bark: greyish brown, with deep ridges	

The crack willow gets its name because its twigs snap easily. It grows near rivers and streams. The twigs fall into the water and float away. Eventually the twigs take root in the riverbank and grow into new trees. The crack willow looks like the white willow but has darker leaves.

▶ *Old crack willow trees sometimes have hollow trunks.*

The catkin of the crack willow is thinner and longer than the catkin of a pussy willow. ▲

Aspen

Scientific name: *Populus tremula*	Native
Height: up to 20 metres	
Bark: smooth, greyish-brown	

The aspen has a thin trunk that bends in the wind. It has round-shaped leaves with wavy edges. The leaves have a long stalk which means they tremble and shake when the wind blows. They make a soft rustling sound. The aspen grows male and female flowers on different trees. The aspen will grow almost anywhere but it prefers moist soil.

▲ *These aspen leaves turn yellow in autumn.*

▲ *The aspen is a member of the poplar family.*

White poplar

Scientific name: *Populus alba*	Introduced
Height: up to 20 metres	
Bark: smooth, pale grey or white, with rows of diamond-shaped black marks	

The white poplar got its name because its leaves look almost white. The young leaves are covered with a thick layer of white hairs. This makes them soft to touch. Eventually, these hairs disappear from the top of the leaf but because they stay on the bottom the tree still looks pale.

The white poplar was introduced to Britain from Europe. It grows best in the south of England where it is warmer.

◀ *White poplar leaves vary in size and shape. Some leaves look triangular. Others have five rounded parts called lobes.*

Grey poplar

Scientific name: *Populus x canescens*	Introduced
Height: over 30 metres	
Bark: grey or pale grey, with rows of diamond-shaped black marks	

The grey poplar is a hybrid. It is a cross between the white poplar and the aspen. It grows much taller than both of these trees. Its leaves are very unusual. Some leaves look like aspen leaves. Other leaves look like white poplar leaves.

▼ *Can you see the mistletoe growing on the branches of this grey poplar?*

Black poplar

Scientific name: *Populus nigra*	Native
Height: up to 35 metres	
Bark: dark, coarsely ridged	

The black poplar is named after its dark bark. You can also tell it apart from other poplars because it has rough lumps growing on its trunks. These bumps are called burrs. The black poplar has heavy branches that grow low on its trunk. Its leaves are almost heart-shaped with a wavy edge.

The black poplar grows best in wet woods and beside streams and rivers. In the past it was popular but now it is one of Britain's rarest trees. In the 1970s scientists discovered that there were no seedlings to replace the old trees. There were two reasons for this. Firstly, people had stopped planting female trees. This was because the catkins produced a fluff that irritated people's noses and eyes. Scientists also found out that the seeds of the black poplar need silt found near riverbanks to germinate. It was difficult for the black poplar to grow because farmers were using the land near rivers to graze animals instead.

▲ *Like all poplar trees, the black poplar grows quickly.*

Fortunately, these discoveries mean that steps have been taken to save the black poplar. Young trees are being grown and planted in the places where they used to grow. The black poplar used to be most common in southern England. In the past it was planted near villages and farms. Its soft white wood was used for floorboards and making carts.

Lombardy poplar

Scientific name: *Populus nigra var. italica*
Height: about 30 metres
Bark: greyish brown, ridged, with twigs growing right up the trunk
Introduced

The Lombardy poplar is a type of black poplar but it looks very different. Its branches point upwards to create a tall narrow crown. Often, it is used as a windbreak and is planted in rows in parks and fields. Like all kinds of poplar tree it grows very quickly.

▼ *The Lombardy poplar was first brought to Britain from Italy.*

Silver Birch

Scientific name: *Betula pendula*	Native
Height: up to 30 metres	
Bark: white, with black cracks	

Silver birches like light, dry soils. They are found over much of Britain and Europe.

The silver birch got its name from its silver coloured trunk. It is an attractive tree with slender, drooping twigs. Its leaves are small with toothed edges. Each tree has male and female catkins. The female catkins produce seeds. The seeds are contained in dry winged fruits that can be carried by the wind.

Twigs and sticks from the silver birch are used to make the brooms on broomsticks. These traditional types of broom are called besoms. You might know them better as witches' broomsticks.

▲ *The trunks of the silver birch seem to shine like silver in the sun.*

▶ *Male catkins on the silver birch dangle downwards. Female catkins are smaller and stand upright.*

▲ *The seeds from the alder tree float on the surface of water. They are carried by water until they find a place to grow on the riverbank.*

Alder

Scientific name: *Alnus glutinosa*	Native
Height: over 20 metres	
Bark: greyish-brown, with square-shaped cracks	

Alders grow best next to water. The roots of the trees stop the waterlogged soil being washed away. The alder has dark-green leaves. The leaves are round with a notch at the top.

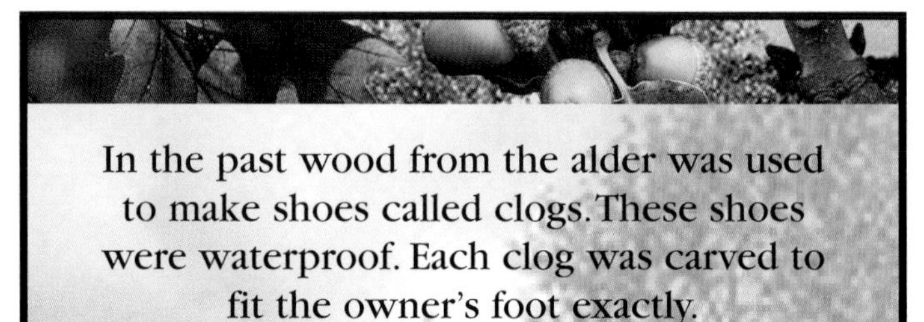

In the past wood from the alder was used to make shoes called clogs. These shoes were waterproof. Each clog was carved to fit the owner's foot exactly.

▲ *Epping Forest and Hatfield Forest in Essex are famous for their hornbeams. In the past, Londoners used its branches for firewood.*

◀ *The male catkins of a hornbeam tree.*

Hornbeam

Scientific name: *Carpinus betulus*	Native
Height: up to 30 metres	
Bark: smooth, mid-grey with vertical brown streaks	

The hornbeam grows in parts of south-east England, Somerset and Wales. The wood from the hornbeam makes good firewood and is used to make charcoal.

The hornbeam has oval and coarsely toothed leaves. It has separate male and female catkins. The hornbeam's seeds grow inside a tiny nut. The nut has a papery, three-lobed 'wing'. These winged nuts can be carried and spread by the wind.

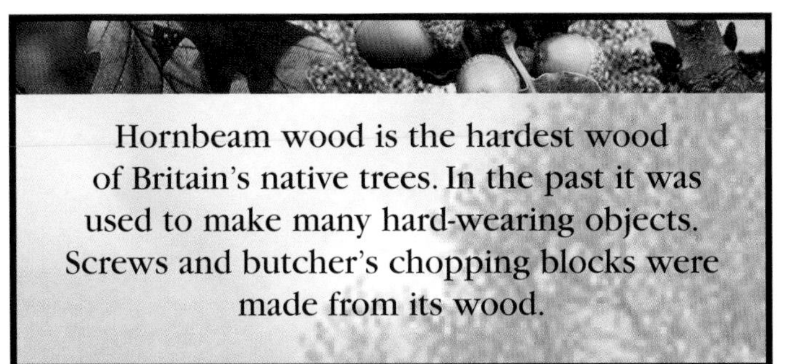

Hornbeam wood is the hardest wood of Britain's native trees. In the past it was used to make many hard-wearing objects. Screws and butcher's chopping blocks were made from its wood.

Hazel

Scientific name: *Corylus avellana*	Native
Height: up to 6 metres	
Bark: smooth, brown	

The hazel is a very common shrub. It produces tasty nuts that can be eaten by humans and animals. Hazel wood is often used to make fencing, hurdles, small poles and firewood. The hazel is also cut back to make hedges. Since it is so useful, the hazel is often cultivated. Its shoots are regularly cut back and harvested. This practice is called coppicing.

▶ *The hazel is one of the most commonly coppiced shrubs.*

Beech

Scientific name: *Fagus sylvatica*	
Height: up to 40 metres	
Bark: smooth, grey	
Native	

The beech grows best in well-drained soil. It is mainly found in southern England. In spring its buds burst open to reveal its pointed oval leaves. By summer the leaves are a rich deep green. When its in full leaf the beech creates a heavy shade.

Its flowers begin to appear when the leaves open. These small greenish flowers are male and female. Beech seeds grow as nuts inside bristly cups. The cups split open when the seeds are ripe. The beech tree only produces seeds every four years. At this time fresh green seedlings carpet the forest floor. Only a few of these will survive and grow into mature trees.

▲ *In the past thin sheets of beech wood were used as a kind of paper.*

▶ *Beech seedlings cover the forest floor.*

Beechwood has been used for making furniture for many centuries. It doesn't smell or taste of anything so it is often used to make kitchen utensils such as rolling pins and wooden spoons.

Sweet chestnut

Scientific name: *Castanea sativa*	Introduced
Height: about 30 metres	
Bark: brown with spiral ridges	

It has large, deeply toothed leaves and prickly husks. Its male catkins look like hairy golden caterpillars.

It produces delicious chestnuts that can be roasted over a fire or made into turkey stuffing.

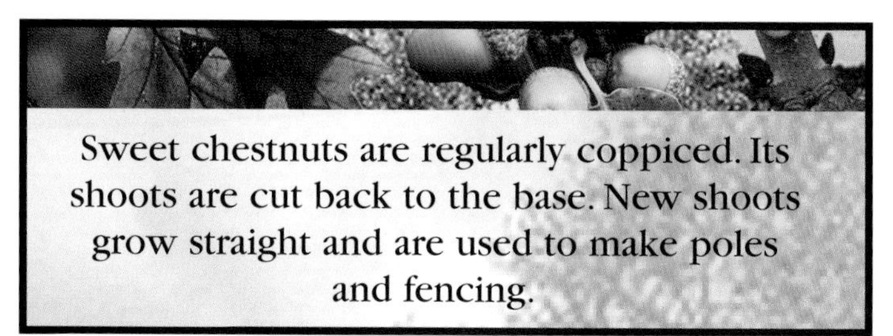

Sweet chestnuts are regularly coppiced. Its shoots are cut back to the base. New shoots grow straight and are used to make poles and fencing.

Inside these prickly husks are the ripe sweet chestnuts. ▲

▼ *The sweet chestnut tree is very tall. Its bark grows in spiral ridges.*

Holly

▼ *In the past people believed it was bad luck to chop down a holly tree.*

▲ *Only the female flowers of the holly grow into berries.*

Scientific name: *Ilex aquifolium*	Native
Height: up to 25 metres	
Bark: smooth, grey with darker marks and small bumps	

The holly tree is easily recognizable because of its dark prickly leaves and bright red berries. It is also the only native broadleaved tree that is evergreen. Each leaf has curvy edges that end in a sharp point or spine. These spines prevent animals such as deer from eating the leaves.

The holly has white flowers that grow in summer. These appear in male and female clusters and are pollinated by insects. The berries appear in October. Each berry contains three or four seeds. The berries are eaten by birds but are poisonous to humans.

In ancient times people put holly in their homes because they believed it guarded against evil spirits.

Common oak

Scientific name: *Quercus robur*	Native
Height: over 30 metres	
Bark: dark grey-brown, rough and cracked	

Oakwood is strong and has many uses. In the past its great timbers were used to make ships or the frames for buildings. These days good quality oak is used for making furniture and rougher wood is used for making fences.

The oak tree is one of the best-loved trees in Britain. Conservation of older trees is considered very important. Oak forest used to cover most of Britain. These were gradually cleared to make farmland. You can still see lots of oak trees in woodlands, parks and gardens.

Two species of oak are native to Britain. The common oak or English oak is the most widespread. In the wetter north and west of Britain, the sessile oak is more common.

The oak is easy to recognize by its long, lobed leaves. It also grows acorns which sit neatly in scaly cups. The acorns on a common oak grow on long stalks. On a sessile oak the acorns don't have a stalk.

Birds and other wildlife enjoy eating acorns.

◀ *You can tell that this is a sessile oak because its acorns have no stalks.*

▼ *In open spaces the common oak has a broad crown. Some oak trees can live for up to 1,000 years.*

▲ *The bark of the holm tree is very dark. It almost looks black from a distance.*

▶ *The acorns of the holm oak sit in a hairy cup. They ripen between May and September.*

Holm oak

Scientific name: *Quercus ilex*	Introduced
Height: up to 28 metres	
Bark: almost black, cracked into thin squares	

The holm oak was introduced to Britain from southern Europe. They are often found in parks and gardens or along riverbanks in south-west England.

The holm oak is an evergreen tree with dark-green leaves. The edges of the leaves sometimes have small spines. The acorns of the holm oak are smaller than those of the common or sessile oak. They are about 1.8 centimetres long and sit deeply in the cup.

Red oak

Scientific name: *Quercus borealis*	Introduced
Height: up to 25 metres	
Bark: smooth and grey, sometimes with shallow cracks or scattered lumps	

The red oak was brought to Britain from eastern North America. It is easy to tell apart from our native oaks by its leaves. The leaves of the red oak have large pointed lobes. Leaves can reach up to 20 centimetres long. In autumn these leaves turn bright red. Sometimes they change to purple before they fall off the tree. Since it is such a spectacular tree in autumn, the red oak is often planted as an ornamental tree. Its timber can be used for making furniture. It is a solid wood that is also useful for making carts and wheels.

▶ *Many people visit North America just to see the beautiful red oak trees in autumn.*

Sycamore

Scientific name: *Acer pseudoplatanus* **Introduced**

Height: up to 35 metres

Bark: smooth, grey with flaking patches

One of the most common trees originally in Britain is the sycamore. It was brought from central and southern Europe. It is a tough tree that can survive heavy winds, salty coastal air and industrial pollution.

The sycamore is a large tree with big palm-shaped leaves. Each leaf has five toothed lobes, arranged a little like fingers on a hand. Its flowers appear in spring. It is one of the few common trees to be pollinated by insects. Many bees rely upon the sycamore for their pollen.

Sycamore seeds grow in winged fruits, often called 'helicopters'. These fall from the tree in autumn. They spin like the rotor blades of a helicopter. This means they can travel a great distance.

▲ *Sycamore trees create a lot of shade. This can make it difficult for other trees to grow nearby. For this reason, woodland managers try to limit the number of sycamores they plant.*

◀ *The sycamore flowers are small and pale green.*

The best sycamore wood is very expensive. It is used for fine furniture and the best violins.

▶ *Each half of the field maple fruit contains one seed.*

Field maple

Scientific name: *Acer campestre* **Native**

Height: up to 25 metres

Bark: greyish-brown, with fine cracks and ridges

The field maple is one of the most beautiful native trees in Britain. They are mostly found in central, southern and eastern England. Its leaves are divided into five lobes. When they open in spring the leaves are pinkish red. Eventually they turn green but in autumn they change from yellow to red and purple.

◀ *The field maple has colourful leaves in autumn. Its leaves are like sycamore leaves but smaller.*

Ash

Scientific name: *Fraxinus excelsior*

Height: up to 42 metres

Bark: pale brownish-grey, ridged

Native

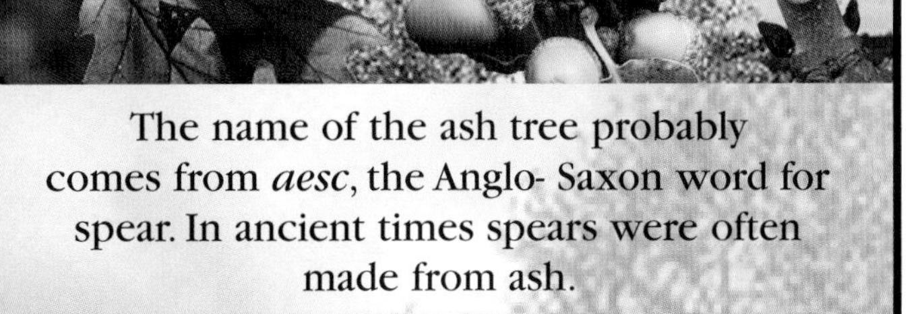

The name of the ash tree probably comes from *aesc*, the Anglo- Saxon word for spear. In ancient times spears were often made from ash.

The ash is a tough tree that will grow almost anywhere. It grows all over Britain but is most common in the wet, limestone soils in the north.

This large tree is one of the last to open its leaves in spring. It is also one of the first trees to shed its leaves in autumn. Its leaves are pinnate. This means it has one central stem and about 9 to 13 small leaflets. These leaflets are arranged in two rows along the stem with one leaflet at the tip. Its small green flowers open in April before the leaves. Its seeds are contained in winged fruits that are carried by the wind.

▶ *This mature ash tree has an uneven crown.*

▼ *It is easy to identify the ash tree in winter. It is covered with black velvety buds.*

Ash wood is tough but it bends. It is also strong and doesn't split easily. This means it is excellent for making handles of tools such as hammers and axes. It is also used to make sports equipment like hockey sticks, snooker cues and oars.

Wild privet

Scientific name: *Ligustrum vulgare*	Native
Height: up to 3 metres	
Bark: dark grey, smooth	

Wild privet is a shrub that grows on chalky soils in England. It is also planted in gardens.

Wild privet is partly evergreen which means it keeps some of its leaves through the winter. Its leaves are shiny and green. They are oval, pointed and leathery. Small white flowers open in the summer. The flowers turn into blue-black berries. These are eaten by birds but are poisonous to humans.

▲ *The wild privet's flowers have a strong, unpleasant scent. This attracts all kinds of insects.*

Box

Scientific name: *Buxus sempervirens*	Native
Height: up to 7 metres	
Bark: pale brown or grey, cracked into small squares	

Box is often shrubby but it can grow into a small tree. It is found naturally in only a few parts of southern England. Box grows best on chalky or limy soils. It is also grown in gardens, where it can be cut into neat, evergreen hedges.

Box has small, leathery leaves that are dark-green and shiny on top. Its yellow flowers are small and are pollinated by insects. They open in April and May and develop into bluish-green seed capsules.

▲ *Box is often used in ornamental gardens. It can be cut into neat shapes.*

▶ *Clusters of box flowers appear in April and May.*

Box is very hard. In the past, before plastic was invented, it was used to make pots and mathematical instruments like rulers.

Wych elm

Scientific name: *Ulmus glabra*	Native
Height: up to 42 metres	
Bark: brownish grey, with cracks and furrows	

The wych elm is most likely to be seen in the north and west of Britain. It has a more even-shaped, spreading crown than the English elm and its twigs are smoother.

▶ *Wych elms can catch Dutch elm disease so not many are planted.*

◀ *The fruit of the wych elm has a broad papery wing with a single seed in the middle.*

Elm wood is a hard wood that doesn't split easily. In the past it was used to make furniture, wheels for carts and coffins. Elm wood doesn't rot in water easily either. It was hollowed out to make wooden water pipes. Some of these pipes can last over a hundred years. Elm wood is still used to make floorboards, wooden bowls and butcher's blocks.

English elm

Scientific name: *Ulmus procera*	Native
Height: up to 30 metres	
Bark: dark brown, cracked into square-shaped plates	

In the past elm trees were one of the most common trees in Britain. They were used to make hedgerows and were planted in parks, villages and farms. The English elm was popular because it is a large, majestic tree that grows quickly. It has rough, unevenly shaped leaves and flat, round winged fruit.

In the 1970s Dutch elm disease began to kill thousands of elms. The disease is caused by a deadly fungus spread by tiny beetles.

Underneath the bark of this dead elm you can see the tunnels made by the beetles that spread Dutch elm disease. ▼

▶ *A healthy English elm. Leaves on a diseased tree turn brown before the tree dies.*

London plane

Scientific name: *Plantus x hispanica*	Hybrid
Height: over 30 metres	
Bark: brownish-grey, flakey, with paler patches underneath	

The London plane is a cross between the oriental plane and the American plane. It was first planted in England at the end of the seventeenth century. The London plane can survive high levels of pollution. Dirt washes away from its leaves easily. For this reason it can be planted on busy city streets.

The London plane has large leaves, about 10 centimetres wide. Each leaf has five toothed lobes that are arranged like fingers on a hand. It has male and female flowers. These grow in separate rounded flower heads. The female flower head changes into a round ball of small, seed-containing fruits.

▲ *The London plane has glossy leaves. This means that dirt and soot wash off them easily.*

Common lime

Scientific name: *Tilia x vulgaris*	Hybrid
Height: up to 46 metres	
Bark: grey, with ridges and burrs at the base	

The common lime is a cross between two native species of lime, small-leaved lime and the large-leaved lime. The common lime is bigger and more common than both of these species. It is often found on pavements and in gardens in towns and suburbs. It can grow very big so it is regularly pruned.

Lime leaves are heart-shaped and have toothed edges. The flowers smell very sweet and are pollinated by bees. The flowers hang in bunches and ripen into small round nut-like fruit in September. The papery leaf-like bracts hang above the nuts. And this helps them fall through the air and disperse.

▲ *Lime trees were often planted along the drives leading up to stately homes. This avenue of limes can be found at Clumber Park, Nottingham.*

Horse chestnuts

Scientific name: *Aesculus hippocastanum*	Introduced
Height: up to 39 metres	
Bark: dark-grey, cracking into rough plates	

◀ *The seed of the horse chestnut is called a conker. It has a spiky case.*

▲ *In the open, horse chestnuts can grow up to 39 metres high.*

▼ *The sticky bud of the horse chestnut opens to reveal fresh green leaves.*

The horse chestnut is one of the most popular trees in the towns and countryside of Britain. It was introduced to Britain in 1629 from the Balkans, in south-east Europe. It is common in parks and large gardens.

The horse chestnut has compound leaves that are made up of 5–7 leaflets. These grow like fingers from the tip of the leaf stalk. It is a huge tree that is impressive in full bloom. In May, its broad, spreading crown is covered in spikes of pink-blotched white flowers. These look a little like large candles. In September the horse chestnut is heavy with shiny brown seeds known as a conkers.

The pale cream wood of the horse chestnut is not very strong. It is rarely used except for small items like toys, boxes and brush handles.

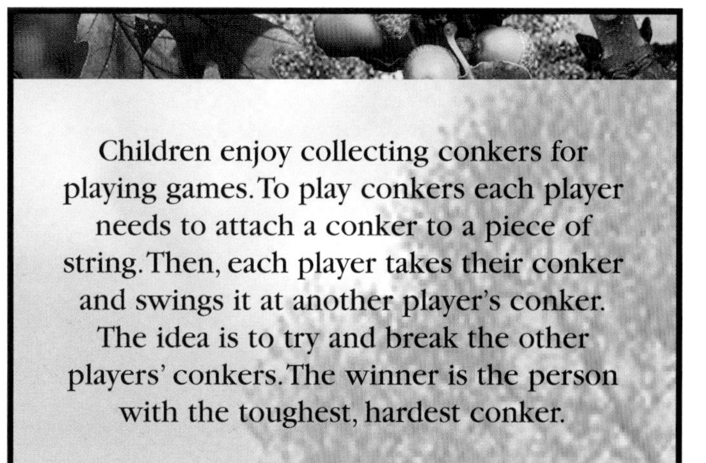

Children enjoy collecting conkers for playing games. To play conkers each player needs to attach a conker to a piece of string. Then, each player takes their conker and swings it at another player's conker. The idea is to try and break the other players' conkers. The winner is the person with the toughest, hardest conker.

Hawthorn

Scientific name: *Crataegus monogyna and Crataegus laevigata*	Native
Height: about 10 metres	
Bark: dark-brown, cracked into narrow rectangles	

Hawthorn is one of the most widespread woody plants of Britain. It can grow as a tree or a shrub.

There are two kinds of hawthorn that are native to Britain. They are both called hawthorn, although one is more correctly called midland hawthorn. These two species often cross with each other to make a hybrid tree.

Hawthorns have sharp thorns on their stems. They have small, dark-green leaves divided into lobes. In May and June the hawthorn is covered in white or pink flowers. By autumn the flowers have ripened into red berries. Each berry contains one or two hard seeds. The hawthorn grows very quickly for the first 15 years.

▲ *The hawthorn has pretty little flowers with round petals.*

◀ *The berries of the hawthorn are called haws. By winter the haws have usually been eaten by birds and mice.*

The hawthorn is also called May tree, May bush and May flower. This is because it is in full flower during May.

Rowan

Scientific name: *Sorbus aucuparia*
Height: up to 18 metres
Bark: pale greyish-brown, scaly
Native

The rowan is sometimes called mountain ash. It is small and attractive so it is popular in gardens.

The rowan has compound leaves that are divided into 9–15 leaflets. The leaflets are arranged in two rows, with a single leaflet at the tip. Each leaflet is oblong in shape, with toothed edges.

◀ *The rowan is widespread in Scotland. This is because it can grow higher up the mountain than any other tree.*

◀ *In May the Rowan is covered in creamy-white flowers. By August these have ripened into orange-red berries as seen in the main picture.*

Blackthorn

Scientific name: *Prunus spinosa*	Native
Height: up to 4 metres	
Bark: nearly black	

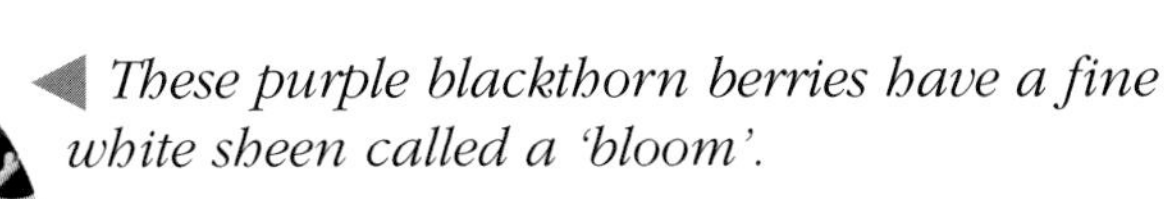

◀ *These purple blackthorn berries have a fine white sheen called a 'bloom'.*

▼ *Blackthorn spreads quickly using suckers. These are shoots that grow up from the roots of the main plant.*

The blackthorn is one of the most common shrubs in Europe. It grows almost anywhere and spreads easily. You can see it in hedges, on the edge of woodlands and wasteland.

The blackthorn has thorns along its stems. Its white flowers often appear before the leaves open. In autumn, the blackthorn is covered in blue-black berries called sloes. These berries are not poisonous to humans but they taste very sour and are nearly impossible to eat.

▲ *The crab apple often grows in hedgerows. Later in the year its branches will be weighed down with lots of tiny crab apples.*

Crab apple

Scientific name: *Malus sylvestris*	Native
Height: up to 10 metres	
Bark: greyish-brown, scaly	

The crab apple is a small thorny tree. It grows mostly on the edges of woods, or in hedgerows and other lightly wooded places.

The crab apple has spiny twigs and oval leaves. By March it is covered in blossom. Each flower has five white petals flushed with pink. Its fruits look like eating apples, but at just 3 centimetres across they are much smaller. These tiny apples taste very sour but can be used for making jam or wine. The seeds (the pips) of the tree are in the core at the centre of the apple.

◀ *Crab apple flowers are pollinated by bees.*

Cherry laurel

Scientific name: *Prunus laurocerasus*	Introduced
Height: up to 10 metres	
Bark: dark, slightly rough	

The cherry laurel comes from south-east Europe and south-west Asia. It was first planted in Britain in the sixteenth or seventeenth century. It is a fast-growing evergreen and is often used in garden hedges or shrubberies.

The cherry laurel has oblong leaves that are thick, leathery and dark-green. Other plants can't grow underneath a cherry laurel because it creates such a deep shade. The cherry laurel bears white flowers in April to June. Purple-black berries ripen in late summer. Birds feast on the berries but they are poisonous to humans and livestock.

▲ *The cherry laurel is usually a thick shrub. It can grow into a tree if it is not clipped or pruned.*

Whitebeam

Scientific name: *Sorbus aria*	Native
Height: up to 23 metres	
Bark: grey, developing shallow scales	

The whitebeam is a small tree with light green leaves. Often it stands out from other trees because of its light colour. It grows well in chalky, limy or sandy soils. It can be found in the wild in parts of southern Britain and Ireland.

The whitebeam has oval leaves that are edged with rounded teeth. They look very pale when they first open. This is because they are covered in white hairs. Eventually, the hairs from the top of the leaves fall off. The whitebeam has flower heads containing tiny white flowers. It has bright-red berries in September. These berries can be made into jam and wine. The brown wood of the whitebeam is fairly hard. It is used to make furniture and tool handles.

▲ *Whitebeam berries can be made into jam and wine.*

◀ *The pale-green leaves of the whitebeam: they make the tree stand out against other trees with darker leaves.*

Wild cherry

Scientific name: *Prunus avium*	Native
Height: up to 31 metres	
Bark: purplish, developing black cracks	

The wood of the wild cherry tree is very good quality. It has a beautiful reddish-brown colour. This means it is used to make furniture, veneers and musical instruments. When it is used as fire wood it smells of blossom.

The wild cherry produces dark-red fruits called cherries. These fruits are too sour for humans. However, the trees that produce sweet cherries to eat are descended from wild cherry trees.

The wild cherry grows in hedgerows, parks, gardens and on the edge of woods. The oval leaves are dark green with a sharply toothed edge. Small white flowers are arranged in clusters along the shoots. The cherries appear in June.

◀ *The wild cherry in full blossom. Most trees are tall and thin. This old tree has spread out as it has grown.*

Common or wild pear

Scientific name: *Pyrus communis*	Introduced
Height: up to 20 metres	
Bark: dark-brown or black, deeply cracked into small squares	

The common pear tree produces little fruits called pears. These fruits are rounder and smaller than the pears you buy at the supermarket. The pears you eat come from a tree that is descended from the common pear tree.

The leaves of the common pear tree are oval and shiny, with finely toothed edges. It has small white flowers that attract bees. The seeds of the tree are found inside the core of the fruit.

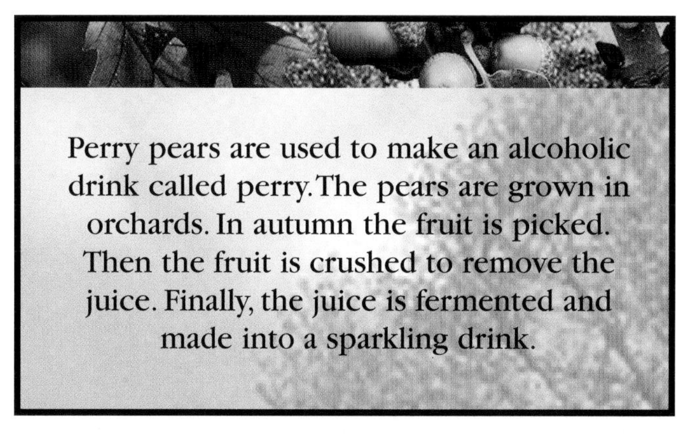

▶ *There are three groups of cultivated pear trees: dessert pears, cooking pears and perry pears. They are all descended from the common pear tree.*

Spindle

Scientific name: *Euonymus europaeus*	Native
Height: 5-8 metres	
Bark: grey, smooth	

The spindle tree got its name because its wood is made into spindles. Spindles are used to wind wool after it has been spun. In the past spindles were occasionally used as Christmas trees.

Spindle is most common as a shrub in a hedgerow but it can also grow into a small tree. It is widespread on chalky soils in Britain. Its oval leaves are narrow and pointed at the tip. In autumn the leaves turn from green to red. Its tiny greenish flowers are about 1 centimetre wide. These ripen into bright-pink fruits. Each fruit has four lobes containing four orange seeds.

▶ *The seeds and fruits of the spindle are poisonous.*

▲ *The flowers of the spindle are small and easy to miss.*

Guelder rose

Scientific name: *Viburnum opulus*	Native
Height:up to 4 metres	
Bark: grey	

The guelder rose is a shrub that grows in woods and hedges. It especially likes damp soil. It is often planted in gardens because it looks attractive and has lots of fragrant flowers.

The guelder rose has lobed leaves. These turn deep red or yellow in autumn. Its rounded flower heads are made up of many flowers. There are large white flowers on the outside of the flower head. Then on the inside there are smaller creamy-yellow flowers. Only the small flowers produce fruit. In autumn the shrub is filled with juicy red berries. Each berry contains a single seed. The leaves, bark and berries of the guelder rose are poisonous to humans.

◀ *The flowers of the guelder rose are attractive to hover flies and other insects.*

Buckthorn

Scientific name: *Rhamnus cathartica*	Native
Height: up to 8 metres	
Bark: split, scaly, tinged orange	

▶ *Buckthorn branches are covered in sharp thorns.*

Buckthorn is a thorny shrub that grows in hedgerows and open woodlands. Buckthorn has oval, pointed leaves that grow opposite each other up the stem. Its stems are often thorny. The flowers of the buckthorn are yellow-green in colour. The flowers ripen into purplish-black berries. Each berry has between two to four seeds.

The berries and bark of buckthorn are poisonous. In the past people used them to cure constipation. However, it usually made them violently sick and caused diarrhoea.

▲ *The timber from the dogwood is very strong.*

Dogwood

Scientific name: *Cornus sanguinea*	Native
Height: up to 4 metres	
Bark: dark-red at first, becoming brown with age	

Dogwood is a shrub that grows wild in hedges and woodlands. It is most common where the soil is chalky or limy clay. Dogwood is also planted in gardens. This is because in winter the bare new shoots turn a beautiful deep-red colour.

The dogwood has oval, pointed leaves. These are arranged opposite each other along the stems. In June and July its small white flowers appear. They are arranged in rounded clusters at the tip of the shoots. Small purplish-black fruits ripen from August to October. These taste bitter so they are not good to eat. Each fruit contains one seed.

◀ *The flowers of the dogwood attract insects, which pollinate them.*

▲ *The bright pink flowers of the rhododendron are very striking.*

Rhododendron

Scientific name: *Rhododendron ponticum*	Introduced
Height: up to 5 metres	
Bark: brown, becoming cracked with age	

The rhododendron is a broad, spreading, evergreen shrub. It was introduced to Britain in the eighteenth century. The Victorians used it as an ornamental shrub for parks and gardens. It grows very well on acidic, peaty or sandy soils. It spreads rapidly, both by seeds and by suckers. The shrub can be a nuisance because native plants die in the rhododendron's shade.

The rhododendron has narrow oblong leaves that feel leathery. In early to mid-summer the shrub is covered in large, domed flower heads. Each head is made up of many bell-shaped, pinkish flowers.

Elder

Scientific name: *Sambucus nigra*	Native
Height: up to 10 metres	
Bark: brownish-grey, furrowed and cork	

The elder is a shrub or small tree. It often grows in hedgerows and woods. It is a pretty tree that is prized for its flowers and fruits. These are used to make cordials, jams and wine.

The elder has compound leaves. These are divided into 3–7 leaflets. The elder has large flat flower heads, the creamy white flowers appear in late May and early June. Its purple-black berries ripen in late summer.

The seeds of the elder are spread by birds that have eaten the berries. ▲

▲ *The elder has sweet-smelling flowers.*

Gorse

Scientific name: *Ulex europaeus*	Native
Height: up to 2.5 metres	
Bark: greyish	

◀ *Gorse is pollinated by insects.*

▼ *A bank of gorse in full flower smells like coconut.*

Gorse is a small prickly shrub. Each stem is covered with branched, bluish-green spines. Only young gorse plants have leaves. These drop off as the plant gets older. Gorse flowers are bright yellow. They open most of the year but are at their best in June. The seeds of the gorse develop in black pods.

Broom

Scientific name: *Cytisus scoparius*	Native
Height: up to 2.5 metres	
Bark: green, ridged	

Broom is a small upright shrub. Its flowers are yellow, with red or mauve patches. Its seeds are found inside black pods. When the pods split open, the seeds shoot out.

▲ *Broom leaves are made up of three small leaflets.*

◀ *Broom belongs to the same family as gorse, but it does not have any sharp spines.*

Laburnum

Scientific name: *Laburnum anagyroides*	Introduced
Height: up to 8 metres	
Bark: smooth, dark-green, becoming brown	

The laburnum tree was introduced to Britain from central and southern Europe in 1560. It is a small, deciduous tree that grows well in gardens. It has compound leaves that are divided into three leaflets. In May the tree is covered in bright yellow flowers that hang down in long chains. The laburnum has brown seed pods. Its seeds are highly poisonous to humans.

◀ *The laburnum is also called 'golden rain' because of its cascades of yellow flowers.*

▲ *The timber from the walnut tree is expensive. It can be used to make good quality furniture.*

Walnut

Scientific name: *Juglans regia*	Introduced
Height: up to 24 metres	
Bark: pale-grey and smooth, with widely spaced cracks	

The walnut tree is native to an area that spreads from south-east Europe to south-west China. It was brought to Britain in the sixteenth century. The walnut tree is grown for its tasty nuts and for its excellent timber. It has long compound leaves with 3–9 leaflets. Male flowers grow on catkins. The female flower grows at the tip of a young shoot.

Cider gum or eucalyptus

Scientific name: *Eucalyptus gunnii*	Introduced
Height: up to 30 metres	
Bark: peeling in strips of pinkish-brown, grey underneath	

The eucalyptus tree was introduced to Britain from Australia. In Australia there are 500 different kinds of eucalyptus. The evergreen cider gum tree is tough enough to survive in the British climate. It is sometimes grown in parks and gardens. Eucalyptus has distinctive young leaves. These are round and pale bluish-grey in colour. They are often used in flower arrangements.

▶ *Older eucalyptus leaves are spear-shaped and are darker in colour than young leaves.*

Magnolia

◀ *The blooms on this magnolia tree are cup-shaped. They are white, pink and purple in colour.*

Scientific name: *Magnolia x soulangiana* **Hybrid**

Height: up to 7.5 metres

Bark: blackish-grey

The many different species of magnolia were brought to Britain from Asia and North American. The magnolia is a small tree or shrub. In spring it is covered in large, attractive flowers. Unfortunately, they can be killed off if there is a frost. The bull bay is a popular evergreen magnolia tree from south-eastern North America. Its flowers have a strong, sweet fragrance.

Butterfly bush or buddleia

Scientific name: *Buddleia davidii* **Introduced**

Height: up to 5 metres

Bark: grey

▶ *The flowers of the buddleia are rich in nectar making them attractive to butterflies and bees.*

The buddleia is a shrub that originally came from China. Its strongly scented flowers attract many butterflies. This is how it got its other name, the butterfly bush. The buddleia is semi-evergreen. It has bluish-green, lance-shaped leaves. Some of these stay on the plant all year round. The buddleia spreads easily and is common on patches of wasteland.

▲ *Juniper survives harsh weather. This tree's trunk has been twisted by the wind.*

Common juniper

Scientific name: *Juniperus communis*

Height: up to 10 metres

Bark: reddish-brown, shredding

Native

▲ *The cones of the juniper tree have an aromatic smell when they are crushed.*

Common juniper is one of three conifers native to Britain. It rarely reaches its full height in Britain and is usually a low-growing shrub. It has short, needle-like leaves. These needles can be very stiff and sharp on trees found in chalky and lime areas. Needles on trees growing on high ground are much softer. Common juniper has small, round cones. These measure about 1 centimetre across. Each cone contains 1–6 seeds.

▲ *Birds like to eat the red seeds on the yew tree. The seeds are spread in their droppings.*

▶ *This yew tree in Powys, Wales is believed to be at least 2,000 years old.*

Yew

Scientific name: *Taxus baccata*	Native
Height: up to 28 metres	
Bark: scaly, patches of reddish-brown and purplish-brown	

In Britain the yew is one of three native conifers. Its leaves or needles are flat and narrow. They are dark-green above, with two paler lines underneath. The yew does not have a woody cone like many other conifers. Its seeds sit in a fleshy pink cup called an aril. Yews might have a single upright trunk. Many older yews have leaning trunks or have grown more trunks.

There is a great deal of folklore and superstition about the yew. In the past it was a symbol of immortality. Ancient people planted yews near burial grounds. Today you can often see yew trees in graveyards. Some people thought the yew was a symbol of death. Perhaps this is because the leaves, seeds and bark are extremely poisonous and can cause death.

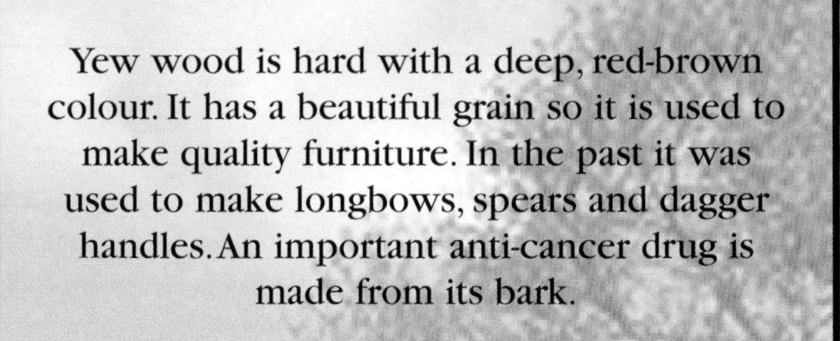

Yew wood is hard with a deep, red-brown colour. It has a beautiful grain so it is used to make quality furniture. In the past it was used to make longbows, spears and dagger handles. An important anti-cancer drug is made from its bark.

Scots pine

Scientific name: *Pinus sylvestis*	Native
Height: up to 36 metres	
Bark: lower trunk: grey and scaly; upper trunk: light-orange or pinkish	

The Scots pine is an evergreen conifer. It grows naturally in the Scottish highlands. In all parts of Britain you will find it growing as an ornamental tree in parks and gardens. It is also planted on plantations for its timber.

It is easy to identify a Scots pine by its trunk. The lower part of the trunk is grey. The upper part of the trunk is a rust-red colour. There is no other pine tree like this. Scots pine leaves are blue-green needles. These are about 2–8 centimetre long. Its winged seeds grow inside cones. A ripe cone is woody and greyish brown. It measures between 2.5–6 centimetres long.

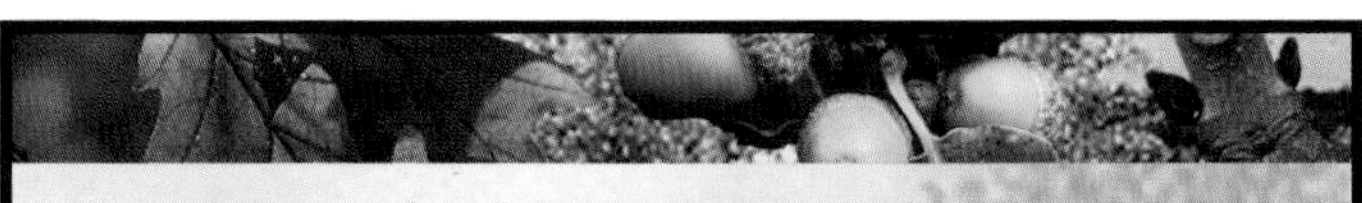

Wood from the Scots pine is light but strong. It is used for furniture, telegraph poles and wood pulp for paper.

▲ *Young Scots pines have straight trunks and a conical crown. Older trees have more spreading crowns.*

◀ *The cones of the Austrian pine are about 5–7.5 centimetres long. They can stay on the tree for several years.*

Austrian pine

Scientific name: *Pinus nigra*	Introduced
Height: up to 42 metres	
Bark: blackish-brown, ridged and scaly	

The Austrian pine is native to western Europe through to Asia. It is an evergreen conifer. This tall tree is often planted in parks and gardens. It also makes a good shelter belt. This means it is used to protect buildings or fields of crops from the wind. Unlike many conifers, it will grow on chalky soils.

The Austrian pine's trunk is almost black. It has dark-green leaves that measure about 8–12 centimetres long. Its woody cones are similar to those of the Scots pine but they are slightly larger.

Norway spruce

Scientific name: *Picea abies* **Introduced**

Height: up to 46 metres

Bark: reddish-brown becoming purplish, cracked into small plates

The Norway spruce is the tree most often used as a Christmas tree in Europe and North America. It is a fast-growing tree that can grow to an enormous height. Even when it is very tall, it keeps its Christmas-tree shape. It has dense whorls of branches growing low on the trunk and a crown that tapers to a point.

Spruces have much shorter, stiffer needles than pines. The needles of the Norway spruce are just 1–2 centimetres long, ending in a point. Each needle stays on the tree for 5–7 years. Spruce cones aren't as hard as pine cones. They also look rounder in shape.

The Norway spruce is also a very useful tree for timber. In the timber trade it is called 'whitewood' and 'white deal.' It is used to make boxes, paper pulp and for chipboard. In the past it was even used to make spruce beer.

▶ *New shoots and needles of a Norway spruce.*

In the past the Norway spruce was the most popular Christmas tree in Britain. These days you can buy silver fir trees from Europe and the grand and noble fir trees from North America. They are becoming more popular because they do not shed their needles so easily.

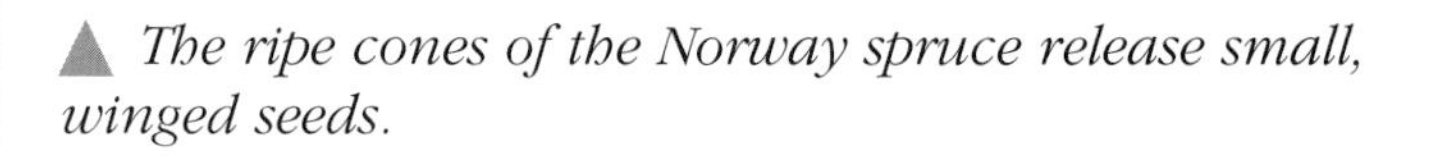

▲ *The ripe cones of the Norway spruce release small, winged seeds.*

Larch

Scientific name: *Larix decidua*	Introduced
Height: up to 46 metres	
Bark: greenish-grey, smooth, becoming cracked	

The larch is a deciduous conifer. It is an attractive tree with a narrow, cone-shaped crown. Its twigs droop down from whorled branches. In autumn, the narrow larch leaves turn golden-yellow and fall. The larch has small, egg-shaped cones. At first they are bright pinkish-red. They take a year to ripen and turn brown. The cones often remain on the tree for much longer, even after all the seeds have blown away.

The larch is often grown in plantations. Its timber is used for outdoor joinery and woodwork.

▲ *The larch is one of the few deciduous conifers.*

▶ *The young cones of the larch are sometimes called larch 'roses'.*

▶ *The Douglas fir often grows to about 85 metres tall in North America.*

▼ *Douglas fir cones measure 5–11 centimetres.*

Douglas fir

Scientific name: *Pseudotsuga menziesii*	Introduced
Height: up to 58 metres	
Bark: purplish-black, with deep, brown cracks	

The Douglas fir originally came from the west coast of North America. It is one of the tallest trees growing in Britain. Its needles are soft and bright green, with two white bands underneath. Its fir cones are unlike those of other conifers. Each wood scale has a three-pronged, papery bract on its outer surface.

Timber from the Douglas fir tree was traditionally used to make masts for sailing ships. Today it is used for heavy-duty construction such as bridge-building.

Cedar of Lebanon

Scientific name: *Cedrus libani*	Introduced
Height: up to 40 metres	
Bark: dark-grey, with small, scaly ridges and short cracks	

The cedar of Lebanon is a majestic tree with a large spreading crown. In the past it was often planted on the lawns of large country houses. Its huge branches arch out low on the trunk. Its leaves are dark-green needles that grow in whorls. The cones are smooth and egg-shaped. They are covered with a sticky white resin. The resin has a pleasant smell but it can be difficult to wipe off your fingers. This resin protects the cones from insect attack. The cones usually break up when they fall from the tree.

▲ *The cedar of Lebanon originally came from the Middle East.*

Atlas cedar

Scientific name: *Cedrus atlantica*	Introduced
Height: up to 39 metres	
Bark: dark-grey, cracked into large plates	

▶ *The cones of the Atlas cedar are made up of overlapping scales.*

Atlas cedars come from the Atlas Mountains of North Africa. They are often planted in large gardens, churchyards and other public places. The most popular kind is the Blue Atlas Cedar with its silvery-blue needles.

Deodar cedar

Scientific name: *Cedrus deodara*	Introduced
Height: up to 37 metres	
Bark: brownish-grey, cracked into small plates	

The deodar cedar comes from the Himalayan Mountains. It is similar to the Atlas cedar but the tips of its shoots droop slightly. It also has longer needles than the Atlas cedar. When it is young, the deodar cedar has a silvery appearance.

◀ *The deodar cedar looks at its best on large sweeping lawns.*

Lawson's cypress

Scientific name: *Chamaecyparis lawsoniana*

Height: up to 41 metres

Bark: purplish-brown, flaky

Introduced

Lawson's cypress originally came from western North America. It grows into a very tall tree with a flame-shaped crown. The branches often grow right down to the ground and hide most of the trunk. Its leaves are like green scales that are pressed closely to the shoots, to make a flattened spray. The cones are spherical and much smaller than those of pines or spruces.

▶ *The cones of Lawson's cypress are less than 1 centimetre wide.*

▲ *The Lawson cypress has attractive glossy leaves.*

Leyland cypress

Scientific name: x *Cupressocyparis leylandii* **Hybrid**

Height: up to 34 metres

Bark: reddish-brown, shallow cracks

The Leyland cypress is a hybrid between two other kinds of cypress. Both of these trees come from North America. The hybrid was produced when these two trees were planted close together in the nineteenth century. The Leyland cypress became popular because it grew quickly. These days, people can have mixed feelings about it. The young trees are often planted as a hedge around gardens and if they are left untrimmed they form high, dense banks of leaves. These cast deep shade over neighbours' houses and gardens.

◀ *The Leyland cypress can be grown into a wind break.*

Monterey cypress

Scientific name: *Cupressus macrocarpa* **Introduced**

Height: up to 37 metres

Bark: brown and ridged

The Monterey cypress comes from Monterey Bay in California, North America. On the coast of southern England it often grows as a small gnarled hedge. Inland, it grows much taller and straighter. As it gets older the crown of the tree becomes more irregular and spreading. The Monterey cypress has small scale-like leaves. These leaves grow on bushy shoots. The cones are about 4 centimetres wide.

▶ *The Monterey cypress is often planted in parks and public places.*

Wellingtonia

Scientific name: *Sequoiadendron giganteum*

Height: up to 50 metres

Bark: reddish-brown, very thick, spongy and fibrous

Introduced

◀ *The wellingtonia has egg-shaped cones. These measure about 7.5 centimetres long.*

The wellingtonia originally came from North America. The wellingtonias of California are amongst the tallest and oldest trees in the world. The first wellingtonias were brought to Britain in 1853. They were often planted in country estates.

Wellingtonia has bright-green, scale-like leaves. The points of each leaf stick out, making the shoot feel spiky if you run your hand along it from tip to base. The thick, fibrous bark protects the trunk from the forest fires that regularly occur in California.

▶ *Some of the wellingtonias growing in California are believed to be over 2,000 years old.*

Ginkgo

Scientific name: *Ginkgo biloba*	Introduced
Height: up to 30 metres	
Bark: brown, corky, becoming cracked and ridged	

The gingko is also known as the maidenhair tree. It comes from an ancient family of trees and is unchanged since the time of the dinosaurs. Today, the only place it grows wild is in the Tianmu Mountains in China. In Britain, it is planted in parks and gardens.

The gingko is most like a conifer tree yet it is not actually part of the conifer family. Ginkgo leaves are fan-shaped and split into two lobes. In autumn the leaves turn bright yellow before they fall.

▲ *There are separate male and female ginkgo trees.*

Monkey puzzle

Scientific name: *Araucaria araucana*	Introduced
Height: up to 29 metres	
Bark: grey, wrinkled into bands, with circular scars where branches have fallen off	

The monkey puzzle tree is a very decorative tree. It comes from the Andes Mountains in Chile and Argentina. It is a conifer and has leaves with sharp spines. The leaves are triangular in shape and feel thick and leathery. They grow all along the stems and branches of the tree, overlapping each other with their spiny tips. The monkey puzzle has separate male and female trees. The pollen-producing cones are found on the male tree.

▲ *The monkey puzzle got its unusual name because somebody once said that the tree would be a puzzle for any monkey to climb.*

◀ *Monkey puzzle shoots grow from the base of the trunk of an adult tree.*

Common conifers in plantations

Trees are a crop, just like wheat or sugar beet. All over Britain, especially in the west and north of the country, you can see trees being grown in plantations. Some of these trees will take over forty years to grow. Only then, can the wood be harvested. Many plantations are filled with conifers. This is because conifers grow more quickly than broadleaved trees. It is also because the demand for wood and paper pulp is never-ending. Conifers are easily pulped and used to make paper. Spruce is also suitable for making paper.

▲ *The male cone of the noble fir is tiny and red.*

Noble fir

Scientific name: *Abies procera*	**Introduced**
Height: up to 47 metres	
Bark: silvery or purplish grey, with resin blisters, developing cracks	

Noble fir and grand fir (*Abies grandis*) are from North America. The noble fir has dark-green, long narrow needles. These are leathery and blunt at the tip. The grand fir has similar needles but they smell of oranges when they are crushed. The female cone of the noble fir break up on the tree and shed their seeds onto the floor below.

Sitka spruce

Scientific name: *Picea sitchensis*	**Introduced**
Height: up to 55 metres	
Bark: purplish-grey, cracking into small plates	

Sitka spruce comes from western North America. It is the most important tree to the British forestry industry. Much of its timber is used to make paper. Together with the Norway spruce, the sitka spruce makes up half of all conifer wood produced in Britain. It has stiff needles with sharp points. The cones are short and sausage-shaped.

▶ *Sitka spruce grows tall quickly.*

Western hemlock

Scientific name: *Tsuga heterophylla*	Introduced
Height: up to 46 metres	
Bark: brown, becoming shredded and flaked	

Western hemlock leaves are most unusual because they are different sizes on the same shoot. The needles at the top of each shoot are half the length of those running in rows below. The tree has small, hanging cones that measure about 2.5 centimetres long.

◀ *Western hemlocks have a crown shaped like a pyramid.*

Lodgepole pine

Scientific name: *Pinus contorta var. latifolia*
Height: up to 25 metres
Bark: dark-brown
Introduced

Lodgepole pine originally comes from North America. It has bright-green twisted needles. These measure about 6 centimetres long and grow in pairs. The cones are no bigger than 6 centimetres long. There is a long thorn at the tip of each scale.

The lodgepole pine used to make the poles for ▶ *tepees and lodges.*

CONIFER	USE OF WOOD
Noble fir	Pallets, kitchen furniture and other joinery.
Grand fir	Pallets, kitchen furniture and other joinery.
Sitka spruce	Plywood, structural timbers, pallets, boxes and crates, wood pulp for paper.
Western hemlock	Plywood, structural timbers, pallets, boxes and crates, wood pulp for paper.
Lodgepole pine	Plywood, structural timbers, pallets, boxes and crates, wood pulp for paper.

Be a Tree Detective

How do you identify different trees? It is a bit like being a detective. You need to follow the clues. It is a good idea to make notes or sketches of the trees you see. Then you can look them up in this book, or other books about trees.

When you want to identify a tree, first take a look at its size. Make a note of the shape of its crown. Then look at the shape of its leaves. Perhaps you could take a few leaves home with you. Next look at the bark. Is it rough or smooth? If there are any what are the flowers like? If it is an evergreen tree you could look for some cones.

A tree detective should look out for changes to trees all year round. Late summer and autumn are the most interesting times for tree detectives. Many trees are filled with ripe fruit. Some trees are easy to identify by their fruits. The oak tree has its acorns and the horse chestnut has its shiny conkers.

▲ *You can identify a rowan tree by its compound leaves and white flowers.*

▼ *The red oak is easy to spot in autumn. Its leaves turn red, orange and gold.*

▼ *You can identify some trees by their flowers. Many trees have small flowers hanging in catkins.*

▼ *Do not forget to use your nose. These gorse flowers smell of coconut.*

WINTER TWIGS

Deciduous trees look very different in the winter compared to the summer. A tree detective can still find lots of clues to help them identify the tree. Now the leaves have fallen, you can see the shape of the twigs. If you look at the silver birch or the weeping willow, you will be able to see the slender drooping twigs. Oak and the horse chestnut have thicker twigs that point upwards.

Pick up some leafless winter twigs and look at them closely. You may be able to see the scars left when the leaves fell in the autumn. Also look for next year's buds. These will be at the sides and tips of each twig. Inside each bud, the tiny young leaves will be tightly folded. They are protected by the tough bud scales.

LEAF RUBBINGS

To make leaf rubbings, you will need:

- leaves collected from trees and shrubs
- a sheet of card or thick paper
- a sheet of thin white paper
- soft coloured pencils or crayons
- sticky tape

1. Lay a leaf flat on the card.
2. Place the white paper on top.
3. Stick down the edges of the paper with sticky tape.
4. Rub gently over the paper and leaf using a pencil or crayon. An outline of the leaf should appear.
5. At the bottom of the rubbing, write down the name of the tree the leaf came from.

▼ *Birch twigs (on the left of this picture) have small, pointed buds. Horse chestnut twigs (on the right of this picture) have large sticky buds.*

Planting Trees

It is fun to grow trees from seeds. You can collect the seeds yourself. Autumn is the best time to gather seeds. Look out for acorns from oak trees or conkers from horse chestnuts.

Collect winged fruits from ash or sycamore trees. Look for pine cones. Put them in a warm place. When they open, shake out the seeds.

PLANTING A TREE

You will need:

- a flowerpot for each type of seed
- garden soil
- labels

1. Collect some acorns, conkers, and ash and sycamore seeds.
2. Fill each flowerpot with soil. Place the seeds on top. Cover lightly with soil.
3. Label each pot.
4. Dig small holes in an empty area of a flowerbed. Stand each pot inside the holes. Leave the pots all winter.
5. In spring the seedlings will appear. There may be too many seedlings in one pot. Separate the seedlings into a pot each.
6. When the seedlings are big enough plant them in the ground. Do not plant them too close to your house!

▲ *Remember to keep your seedlings well watered.*

◀ ▼ *You will even find tree seeds in city parks. Look out for these seeds: (from left to right) chestnuts, acorns, field maples and pine cones.*

Trees and shrubs make our towns and cities more attractive. They provide homes for birds and small mammals. They also keep our air clean because they trap airborne pollutants.

Look around and see what kinds of trees are planted in our towns and cities. Large, tall trees are often planted in parks and playgrounds. You will see small trees or shrubs growing in shopping areas, car parks, gardens around office blocks or in the centre of roundabouts.

Trees produce thousands of seeds in a lifetime. Only a few of these seeds will sprout and grow into adult trees. Sometimes, the seeds are killed by fungus. Other times the seeds have to compete with too many other seeds and die. Often, the seeds do not land in the right place to grow. The city is not an ideal place for young trees either. Young trees need plenty of water to survive and it can be too hot and dry in the city for them.

Young trees being planted on a housing estate in London.

TELLING THE AGE OF TREES

It is possible to tell the age of a tree by counting the rings on its trunk. You can see these rings when the tree is chopped down. Every year, as the trunk grows thicker, another ring appears. Therefore, each ring equals one year.

In Britain the oldest trees are yews. These can live for over 800 years. Oaks can live up to 500 years. Sweet chestnuts live to about 300 years. Birch trees only live for about 70–100 years.

You can tell how old this damson tree is by counting the rings.

Glossary

Bract A leaf-like layer that often surrounds a flower head or cone.

Bud scales The scales that cover a leaf bud. They protect the leaves until they are ready to open in the spring.

Burrs Rough lumps that grow on the trunks of trees.

Crown The top of a tree – the part made up of spreading branches and leaves.

Cultivated A tree that is planted and grown for a particular purpose. For example, pear trees are often grown for their fruit.

Deciduous A tree that sheds all its leaves in autumn.

Disperse To scatter or spread out.

Fermented A substance undergoes a chemical reaction and is broken down into simpler parts.

Germinate To grow or develop.

Husk The thin, dry outer covering of some types of fruit.

Hybrid A cross between two different species of tree or shrub.

Introduced A tree or shrub that has been planted in a country where it is not found naturally.

Lobe A rounded part of a leaf.

Native A tree or shrub that occurs naturally in a country.

Nutrients Food substances needed in order to grow healthy and strong.

Plantations Areas where large numbers of trees are planted as a crop. These trees are usually harvested for their timber.

Pollination To transfer pollen from one flower to another in order to fertilize the tree.

Silt The sediment of mud and fine sand that is deposited by a river or stream.

Species One of the groups into which trees, plants and other living organisms are divided. For example, the red oak is a species of oak.

Spray A spreading shoot or twig with its leaves or flowers.

Suckers Twiggy shoots that grow up from the roots around the base of a tree.

Whorl A ring of leaves, flowers or branches growing around the stem of a plant.

Further information

Books

Cycles in Nature: Plant Life
by Theresa Greenaway
(Hodder Wayland, 2000)

Eyewitness Explorers: Trees
by Linda Gamlin (Dorling Kindersley, 1999)

Look Closer: Tree Life
by Theresa Greenaway
(Dorling Kindersley, 1998)

Nature and Science: Leaves
by Taylor Burton
(Watts, 1997)

Plants: British Trees, British Plants, How Plants Grow
by Angela Royston
(Heinemann, 1999)

Pocket Guide to Wildlife of Britain and Europe
by Jeanette Harris
(Kingfisher, 1988)

Spotter's Guide: Trees
by P. Holden and E. Harris
(Usborne, 2001)

The Earth Strikes Back: Plant Life
by Pamela Grant
(Belitha, 1999)

Ultimate Sticker Book: Trees and Leaves
(Dorling Kindersley, 2006)

Websites

Forestry Commission:
www.forestry.gov.uk

News from the Forestry Commission, plus lots of ideas about how to get active in your forest.

www.the-tree.org.uk/
Britsh Trees/British_R.htm

Visit this interesting site and discover pictures and interesting facts about British trees.

The Royal Forestry Society:
www.rfs.org.uk

Looks at the A to Z of British trees.

Places to visit

Eden Project, Bodelva, St Austell, Cornwall

Visit the giant domed biomes of the Eden Project. The enormous greenhouses have trees and plants that grow all over the world.

Royal Botanic Gardens, Kew, London

The Royal Botanic Gardens is the largest collection of plants and trees in the world.

Westonbirt Arboretum, Gloucestershire

The National Arboretum at Westonbirt is owned by the Forestry Commission. You will find the eldest, tallest and rarest trees in the country here.

Index

Page numbers in **bold** indicate pictures.